To Know The Unknown

EXPLORING THE ISSUES OF REALITY, CHOICE AND FAITH

Now while Paul was waiting for them at Athens, his spirit was provoked within him as he saw that the city was full of idols. So he reasoned in the synagogue with the Jews and the devout persons, and in the market-place every day with those who happened to be there. Some of the Epicurean and Stoic philosophers also conversed with him. And some said, 'What does this babbler wish to say?' Others said, 'He seems to be a preacher of foreign divinities' — because he was preaching Jesus and the resurrection. And they took hold of him and brought him to the Areopagus saying, 'May we know what this new teaching is that you are presenting? For you bring some strange things to our ears. We wish to know therefore what these things mean.' Now all the Athenians and the foreigners who lived there would spend their time in nothing except telling or hearing something new.

So Paul, standing in the midst of the Areopagus, said: 'Men of Athens, I perceive that in every way you are very religious. For as I passed along and observed the objects of your worship, I found also an altar with this inscription: "To the unknown god." What therefore you worship as unknown, this I proclaim to you. The God who made the world and everything in it, being Lord of heaven and earth, does not live in temples made by man, nor is He served by human hands, as though He needed anything, since He himself gives to all mankind life and breath and everything. And He made from one man every

6/24
£2

TO KNOW THE UNKNOWN
EXPLORING THE ISSUES OF REALITY, CHOICE AND FAITH

ROGER CARSWELL

Authentic
LIFESTYLE

Copyright © 2001 Roger Carswell

First published in 2001 by Paternoster Lifestyle

10 09 08 07 06 05 04   7 6 5 4 3 2 1

This edition first published in 2004 by Authentic Media
9 Holdom Avenue, Bletchley, Milton Keynes, Bucks., MK1 1UQ, UK and
PO Box 300, Carlisle, Cumbria, CA3 0QS, UK
and PO Box 1047, Waynesboro, GA 30830-2047, USA
www.authenticmedia.co.uk

The right of Roger Carswell to be
identified as the Author of this Work has been
asserted by him in accordance with
Copyright, Designs and Patents Act 1988

British Library Cataloguing in Publication Data

A catalogue record for this book is available from the British Library

ISBN 1-85078-530-9

Unless otherwise stated, Scripture quotations
are taken from the English Standard Version
Used by permission. All rights reserved.

Cover design by River

Print Management by Adare Carwin
Printed and bound in Denmark by Nørhaven Paperback

Vincent van Gogh was right when he said, **'You may have a blazing hearth in your soul, and yet no one ever comes to sit by it.'** So I am grateful to my mother, Mrs Rhoda Carswell, as well as Dot, Emma and Ben Carswell, Dr Don Carson and Ken Cowen for their input into this manuscript; to Carol Grugeon for her constructive editorial comments and Hazel Fenwick for typing and re-typing it. I found John Stott's book *The Message of Acts*[1] very helpful, so I am grateful to him for some of the ideas in this book. Thanks too, to you the reader, for sitting by the blazing hearth.

I dedicate this book to the memory of Rev Hagop Sagherian, who took time to patiently explain to me the themes which are in this book. It was with him that, sitting on a log in the mountains of the Lebanon, I put my trust in Christ, who means everything to me.

The fire was kindled.

nation of mankind to live on all the face of the earth, having determined allotted periods and the boundaries of their dwelling place, that they should seek God, in the hope that they might feel their way towards Him and find Him. Yet he is actually not far from each one of us, for

"In Him we live and move and have our being",

as even some of your own poets have said,

"For we are indeed His offspring."

Being then God's offspring, we ought not to think that the divine being is like gold or silver or stone, an image formed by the art and imagination of man. The times of ignorance God overlooked, but now He commands all people everywhere to repent, because he has fixed a day on which He will judge the world in righteousness by a man whom He has appointed; and of this he has given assurance to all by raising him from the dead.'

Now when they heard of the resurrection of the dead, some mocked. But others said, 'We will hear you again about this.' So Paul went out from their midst. But some men joined him and believed, among whom also were Dionysius the Areopagite and a woman named Damaris and others with them.

Acts 17:16-34

The Greeks seemed to have it all worked out. They may not have had web sites and mobile phones, but they lived in a society marked by its progress and culture. Their advancement in the arts and sciences was revolutionary.

But despite the outward success of their civilisation, they still sought answers to some fundamental questions: What is the meaning of life? Is there anything beyond this world? Is there a God?

Whatever your memory of school history lessons, it is indisputable that we cannot escape the past. Henry Ford may have said **'history is bunk'**, but he was forgetting that history tends to repeat itself – what happened in days gone by is re-enacted in the present. The past 2000 years have seen the rise and fall of civilisations and empires, but despite the apparent progress of our society the underlying questions people ask are just the same.

Around 50 AD a man arrived in Athens who claimed to have the answers. He was brought before the Council of the Areopagus – a hallowed institution that ruled on matters of religion and philosophy. Some of those who listened remained sceptical and others were not sure, but some believed what he had to say.

If the basic questions haven't changed, then maybe we can learn from the answers of the past.

THE BACKGROUND

Athens was a magnificent city of the ancient world, famous for the Parthenon and the Areopagus, as well as for its art and architecture. It contained images of Apollo, Jupiter, Venus, Mercury, Baachen, Neptune and Diana, as well as gods made of stone, brass, gold, silver, marble and ivory.

THE WRITER

Dr Luke was a meticulously careful historian who lived in the first century AD and had already written an account of the life of Jesus of Nazareth. So gripped was he by the influence of Christ, that Luke went on to describe the events surrounding the early followers of Jesus – the first Christians.

THE MAIN CHARACTER

One of the big players on the scene was Saul of Tarsus, whom we call Paul. He was devout in his religious convictions. As a member of the strictest group of the Jewish religion, he had persecuted the early Christians as he saw them as a distraction from traditional belief. On his way to Damascus to imprison Christians he had been dramatically confronted by the risen Jesus and had become one of His followers.

THE CONTEXT

For the next 30 years Paul devoted himself to proclaiming Christ across the then-known world. In the course of his travels this Christian missionary arrived in the cultural capital of the world.

Paul would have seen plenty to impress him. He travelled the world on three carefully planned journeys. His aim was to preach the Christian message everywhere. He started churches and saw many people converted to Christ.

THE MOTIVATION

What moved Paul most about Athens was not what the sightseer might gaze at, but men and women living in fear of the idols they had made for themselves. People living and dying without any knowledge of God so stirred Paul that he had to speak out and tell the Athenians about Christ, who had claimed to be **'the resurrection and the life'**, adding, **'He who believes in Me, though he may die, he shall live.'**[2]

Paul was a brilliant academic, linguist, philosopher and theologian; but above all, he was a disciple of Christ. He wanted everyone to hear about Jesus Christ, and he felt he could not just remain silent in Athens. He went first to the Jewish synagogue and reasoned with Jews and some Gentile worshippers concerning Christ. Then he went to the marketplace and talked to whoever happened to be there. He was an enthusiast!

THE IMPACT

Though only one man in a busy city, what Paul had to say about Christ caused a stir. Jesus became the talk of the town. Eventually, the impact of Paul's message, which had been turning the world upside down, led him to be taken to the famed Areopagus to tell the Council there about Christianity.

THE CLIMAX

The architecture of the Areopagus was beautiful. What had previously been a judicial council of legendary importance was now a prestigious place of discussion, debate and the airing of new ideas. Despite the curtailment of its ancient powers it remained influential and had special jurisdiction in matters of morals and religion. Philosophers' theories were weighed and, more often than not, found wanting. It was not the place for the faint-hearted to peddle their ideological wares. Yet not everyone who attended this place of debate was intent on seeking and finding the truth. Its more modern-day equivalent would be the Tiergarten in Berlin, Speaker's Corner in London or a university debating chamber. We have seen the antics of many of our politicians in the House of Commons even when they are making big decisions. In a similar way many of the revered members of the Areopagus were equally light in their attitude to matters of great consequence; but it was still a privilege to be given the opportunity to air any ideas and beliefs to the members there.

THE SETTING

IMAGINE THE SCENE:

Paul was small in stature, probably not very good looking, and possibly had poor eyesight. He belonged to a nation that was universally despised, for even though he was born a Roman citizen, he was also Jewish. Brilliant intellectually, he was multi-lingual, an expert in theological matters and a devoutly religious man. His clothes were probably quite poor and his body showed the hallmarks of abuse and scarring.

Sophisticated, learned lawyers surrounded him. They were 'well heeled' and had the upper hand as far as procedure in debate was concerned. Some of the Areopagus were simply there to mock. They referred to Paul as a 'babbler' and had decided what they thought of him before they even heard him speak. They were the type of people who although constantly discussing new things, and happy to do so, would think, **'We've made up our minds – don't confuse us with the facts.'**

Of course, it is difficult for any of us to be totally objective or even open-minded when it comes to assessing Christianity. We are all subject to the background and influences which affect our minds. Neither the media nor the educational system is sympathetic to the Christian message, so if our opinion of Jesus Christ has been moulded by the soaps, our English or even Religious Education teachers, then it is not surprising that we have a distorted view of Jesus Christ.

Harold Shipman, Britain's worst serial killer, committed suicide in prison in January, 2004. It is thought he may have murdered over 250 people. However, people argued that it would have been impossible for him to have a fair trial after all the prejudicial information given about him in the press. Similarly, when so much in the media portrays Christianity as antiquated, irrelevant and untrue, it needs particular integrity to be objective in assessing the message and its historical evidence.

At that time in history, Christianity was beginning to transform the then-known world. While some had reached a conclusion on who they thought Jesus really was, people still wanted to know more about this man who was making such a great impact on society. Paul was about to present a defence of his belief in Jesus, and his audience gave every impression of being hostile; but the reasons for their hostility varied. Some were cynical, arguing that he was proclaiming a foreign religion. Presumably they felt they were above the simple faith of Paul.

'THERE IS NOTHING IN THE BEGINNING, AND THERE IS NOTHING AT THE END, WITH NOTHING IN THE MIDDLE.'

2ND YEAR GENETICS STUDENT

Two groups of people who listened to Paul were particularly noted by Luke in his historical account – the Stoics and the Epicureans. The Stoics argued that 'fate is god' – *'qué será será'* – 'whatever will be, will be'. The Epicureans were the hedonists of the day. Their motto of life was, 'Eat, drink and be merry, for tomorrow we die.' The Stoics said 'endure life'; the Epicureans 'enjoy life'.

These groups of people were ignorant of the gospel of Jesus Christ. Like us today, they all had their own spiritual needs, but despite their high level of education and their place in society, they were pagans. They had no knowledge of their Creator. Why we are here, where we have come from and where we are going were still the three great unanswered questions for them. The God who was so intimately known by Christians was still alien to them, but even the most dismissive of the Areopagus could not easily overlook the remarkable achievements of the still very young church.

Twenty centuries later, many millions of people in each continent of the world claim to have met with the living Christ in a way that has radically changed their lives. Christians may appear to be in the minority, insignificant in the light of the coverage given to those who are critical of religion, but Christian influence is very real. Historically, Christians have been at the forefront of establishing social equality and dignity for slaves, prisoners, children and factory workers. Christians pioneered early trade unions, orphanages, hospitals, schools, and even the British Labour party! Still today, thousands of Christians choose to live and work in the most inhospitable of environments to bring medical and educational aid to the people among whom they live and work, and to share the gospel with them.

Of course, things have been done by 'the church', which are directly contrary to Jesus' teaching and are an embarrassment to Christians. The Crusades, Inquisition or amassing of wealth is hardly acting in obedience to what Christ taught, and therefore it is unfair to blame Jesus for what people have done, even if it was done in His name.

'IF JESUS WAS GOD, HE WAS STUPID TO ALLOW THE ROMANS TO DO WHAT THEY DID TO HIM.'

TEENAGER

▶ WHO IS THE REAL JESUS? ◀

The success of the early church must have mystified onlookers. Christ Himself must have appeared insignificant to the howling mob that gathered outside Pilate's palace and cried 'crucify Him' only 20 years earlier. Many of that mob had, no doubt, previously heard Christ preach. On several occasions thousands had listened to what Jesus had to say, and it was clear that His teaching was contrary to the usual platitudes of the religious teachers of His day. Jesus spoke with originality and authority. What He had to say radically turned the received opinions of His day upside down. What He taught was far from being politically correct.

Israel in Jesus' day was an enemy-occupied country. The oppressive and powerful presence of Roman soldiers on street corners was intimidating. Despite that, Jesus taught people to 'walk the extra mile' and 'turn the other cheek', and even to love their enemies. His own life demonstrated the principles He was teaching, for no one could accuse Him of saying one thing but doing another. All that He said was all that He lived. For 24/7 there was no sleaze or hypocrisy in His life.

He had healed the sick, raised the dead, cured demoniacs and demonstrated power over nature. Yet, here He was, about to be sentenced to a humiliating death by crucifixion. To see Him with lacerations across His face and on His back would have appeared to some to undermine all He had ever promised. However, that scene of pathos – of Christ crucified and subsequently rising from the dead – was to make a huge impact on the world. Those three days between Jesus' crucifixion and resurrection were to become the most unforgettable in all the world's history.

And precisely because of that, Paul was addressing the Areopagus 20 years later. It was a 'David and Goliath' contest, but the impact of Paul's message was to be great. This was partly because Paul addressed the fundamental issues that explained the drawing power of Christianity.

What Paul outlined to this well-educated though pagan people is exactly the same as the message which can bring people to know God today. Though our age has technological expertise unknown to the people of Athens in 50 AD, in other ways there were striking similarities between them and us.

When the Creator God is excluded or false gods are included in the lives of people, then anything can happen. People lose their dignity and significance. It is well expressed in lines from The Bad Touch *by the Bloodhound Gang:* **'You and me, baby, ain't nothing but mammals; so let's do it like they do on the Discovery Channel.'**

Now, as then, there is a fascination with issues of spirituality. There is an abiding sense of dissatisfaction with materialism as the goal of life, and a disappointment with consumerism as the means of soul satisfaction.

'JESUS SAYING "I HAVE COME THAT THEY MAY HAVE LIFE, AND HAVE IT TO THE FULL" IS EITHER THE HEIGHT OF ARROGANCE OR, I SUPPOSE, TRUE.'

A LEVEL STUDENT

Paul loved people, and his genuine warmth and concern would have been immediately apparent. He was not a political pundit who only appeared before his constituents when he wanted their vote. Nor was he a dry academic who stuck to his point of view and was indifferent about how it affected individuals. In living for God, he loved and lived for other people.

Such was Paul's concern to spread the good news of Jesus Christ that he had already been to the synagogue and market place in Athens to preach Jesus to all the people he could. He wanted everyone to know what Christ had accomplished in His life, His death and His rising again. The leaders of society were just as spiritually needy as ordinary people, and Paul felt obliged to share the message of Christ with them too.

It was the reaction to his work in the marketplace that led to the opportunity to speak to the Areopagus. Some philosophers encountered Paul, heard him preaching and began asking him questions. Eventually they took him and presented him to the Aeropagus, wondering how this Council would react to what he was saying.

THE MESSAGE

No doubt Paul was a formidable orator, but as he spoke to the Areopagus he would not be relying on eloquence, sound bites or pithy phrases. He started with a point of general interest, and sought to grab the attention of his audience, but he believed there was a power to his message that came from God alone.

It was said that there were more gods than people in Athens. Nevertheless, the Athenians were not convinced they had quite covered all the possibilities. So, to hedge their bets, they introduced a further idol inscribed 'to the unknown god'. 'The unknown god' was not Christianity under another, or new age guise. Followers of Christ have never been able to be anonymous Christians, but want to declare and share with others their relationship with God. There are people who are moral and upright in their behaviour, but this does not mean that they are therefore Christians. A real believer knows God personally and wants to make Him known to others. Paul began the defence of his message by declaring that the one they worshipped as an unknown god had revealed Himself to humanity.

He explained about who God is, and what He is like. The Athenians were interested in all things spiritual. They were aware of powers beyond the natural world. They had so many gods they could choose their own religion, so who were they to criticise the choice of others? They felt that everything was legitimate – and yet they knew that there was something missing. That is because, by nature, human beings are worshipping creatures. There is an awareness deep within us all that we are more than a conglomeration of chemicals who live, die, and then rot.

Soon the ambivalence that the Areopagus seemed to have towards all beliefs was to be tested. Tolerance is not necessarily a virtue, nor intolerance a vice – it depends on the object of tolerance or intolerance. Tolerance is a willingness to allow different opinions, but it is not cowardly indifference to that which is wrong, nor an assimilation of everything except the truth. The Athenians were to betray their true colours by mocking what Paul had to say.

To begin with they listened silently as Paul explained that God is the Creator of the world and everything in it. Paul was aware of the Greek belief in ancient mythology about how the world began but, as far as we know, he made no attempt to undermine them scientifically. He knew that any rational being would find it incredible to believe that things were made without a Maker, or the world's amazing design had no Designer. As someone once said, it is easier to believe that the dictionary came about as a result of an explosion in a printing works, than to believe this world came into existence without there being a Creator!

Elizabeth Browning expressed the same idea a little more poetically:

> *And every common bush afire with God;*
> *But only he who sees takes off his shoes*
> *– The rest sit around it and pluck blackberries.*

There is a greatness in our world that humbles us. A wound can be cleansed, stitched and bound by a doctor, but who actually heals it? A watermelon seed expands to 200,000 times its own weight, but from where did it receive such ability? Where did birds learn the wonder of migration? Who put the trillions of stars in space, and yet so perfectly formed the billions of cells which co-operate and form our bodies? Each of these things point to an amazing Creator.

Douglas Adams, author of The Hitchhikers' Guide to the Galaxy *said,*
'Space is big. Really big. You just won't believe how vastly mind-boggling big it is. I mean you may think it is a long way down the road to the chemist, but that's just peanuts to space.' [4]

So there is a dishonesty about atheism. It is too easy to suppress the truth of God by denying that we were created in the image of God. Which of us can say that we have passed through every moment of time and found that God did not intervene in the affairs of history? Or who has gone through all of space and found that God is not there? God has revealed Himself. And one basic way in which He has done so is through the universe around us.

The God who brought all things into being is bigger than anything our small minds can grasp. If the dimensions of the universe leave our minds struggling, how can we comprehend the vastness of its Maker?

Despite the splendour of the Greek temples, Paul insisted none of them was big enough to be a home for Almighty God. Cathedrals and churches may have been built 'for the glory of God' but they cannot contain Him. God is a Spirit, so it is impossible to touch Him. We cannot put God in a laboratory to do scientific tests on Him.

'I KEEP A BHAGADVITA AND A BIBLE ON MY BEDSIDE TABLE, AND CARRY A QURAN IN MY POCKET DURING THE DAY. THEY ARE ALL GREAT BOOKS.'
—POSTGRADUATE COMPUTER SOFTWARE STUDENT

Everywhere in the ancient city there were carved images of gods. By speaking of the living God Paul was, in effect, criticising the idolatry of Athens. By saying God does not live in a temple made with hands, Paul was striking a devastating blow at the religious notions of his listeners.

▶ UNIQUE CHRISTIAN CLAIMS ◀

Today's pluralism is the same philosophy that dominated Athens. The smorgasbord of religion which hates to criticise any differing faith appears a noble goal, but it is unsustainable. All religion cannot be true. Consider the fact, for example, that Muslims believe in one god and Hindus believe in many gods. Either one is right and the other wrong, or both are wrong, but both cannot be right. There has to be a law of non-contradiction.

Apart from Christianity, all religions strive to work their way to God. By works and devotion they seek to please their god. Christianity says that God is too pure for defiled humans to reach, but God has taken the initiative and come down to us in the person of Christ. Jesus has reached down to rescue us.

Jesus made amazing claims. He said *'I am the way, the truth, and the life. No one comes to the Father except by Me.'*[5] If all religions are right then Jesus is right, but if Jesus is right then all other religions are wrong – right? He alone in all the world's religions and political leaders would substantiate the truth of His words by rising from the dead.

All that God has revealed about Himself shows Him to be beyond human comprehension. Therefore, there will always be unanswered questions concerning God. If we could understand all there was to know about God, either He would not be God, or we would not be human! God has told us of His eternal qualities, and eternity will be needed to start to fathom the depths of the uncreated deity.

Time and again throughout the pages of the Bible we read words like, **'God spoke and said...'** This collection of 66 books called the Bible is divided into the Old and New Testaments. It claims to be the written revelation of God to our world. But rather than taking second-hand opinions about it, we can begin to read it and discover that God speaks with authority. The Bible carries its own authenticity.

This library of books has one united theme which reveals God to be all-powerful; inescapable, because He is everywhere; knowing all things, and utterly reliable, because He never changes. Through the Bible we know God to be pure and true, just and loving. Repeatedly God describes Himself as being abundant in mercy and full of compassion. He is not only a God 'out there' but, as Paul said, **'He is not far from each one of us.'**[6] He is the God who may be known by individuals and yet is so vast He will always be beyond complete discovery. It is therefore unreasonable to blame God if there is a stale relationship between an individual and Him.

If one begins to really consider what God is like there will be a sense of awe; while God may be familiar, there cannot be familiarity towards Him. I once briefly met Baroness Thatcher, but while respecting her for her office, I did not bow and worship her – and she will long since have forgotten meeting me! God, however, cannot be met on anything like a level playing field. God is God! He is gloriously full of honour and He knows everything there is to know about each one of us. Because of His own nature He cannot ignore us and does not forget us.

'I AM SURE THERE IS A REASON FOR OUR EXISTENCE, BUT I DON'T THINK I WILL EVER FIND IT, SO WHAT IS THE POINT OF LOOKING?'

1ST YEAR MEDICAL STUDENT

WHAT DOES IT MEAN TO BE HUMAN?

God is the life-giver. He sustains the world. From the dust of the ground He made the first human being, breathing life into him so that he became a 'living soul.'[7] Whether male or female, adult or child, each of us is made as a physical, intellectual, social and spiritual being. We were made in the image of God so that we are both created and creative creatures. We are able to love and hate. We feel joy and sorrow. We know what it is to be hurt, and we can also exhibit kindness and care.

There is a wonderful variety in humanity. Consider how different the Pigmy is from the North American, or the Eskimo from the Mongolian, or the European from the South American, or the Chinese from the African. What a rich kaleidoscope of culture, colour and temperaments! God made each one, and He devised the notion of nations and people groups.

So, human beings are of one origin. All human beings meet on one level before God and one day, as the Bible puts it, both great and small shall appear before God the Judge.[8]

Racial, sexual, cultural or age discrimination are negated by what Paul said to the Athenians. To accuse Paul of sexism, as some have, is nonsense. He clearly believed, as the Bible teaches here and elsewhere, that while individuals have differing roles and responsibilities, each is of equal standing in the sight of God. Later Paul wrote, **'There is neither Jew nor Greek, there is neither slave nor free, there is neither male nor female; for you are all one in Christ Jesus.'**[9] He was teaching what Christ had pioneered by His example of showing respect and dignity to women.

Again Paul was implicitly criticising aspects of the Graeco-Roman world in this. With all their magnificent philosophy and ethics, and their achievements in every realm of art, science and literature, in parts of the world their morality and view of women could not have been lower. The Athenian soldier Demosthenes had written 400 years earlier, **'We have prostitutes for the sake of pleasure. We have concubines for the sake of daily cohabitation. We have wives for the purpose of having children legitimately and of having a faithful guardian of our household affairs.'**[10]

'I HAVE TO ADMIT,
THAT AS I HEAR MORE ABOUT JESUS,
MY CYNICISM IS BEING CHIPPED AWAY.'

1ST YEAR SPORTS SCIENCE STUDENT

Of course, some people are born with a better start and have greater opportunities than others. Nevertheless, there is no place in the gospel for caste systems, nor for accepting or rejecting people on the basis of their economic situation. One of the joys of being involved in the Christian community at large is being with people of all abilities and disabilities, from various continents and cultures. There is an acceptance of each other because we are all sons and daughters of God, who is our Father.

There is a dignity about being human that is ignored at our peril. We were made in the image of God and have been given a place of great honour on the earth.

Dominique Lapierre, in his epic story about Calcutta, The City of Joy, *has a harrowing chapter where he describes how Selima, a slum dweller and mother of three, is persuaded to sell the fourth child whom she is expecting in two months. Selima would receive £120 to have an abortion and then have the prematurely delivered baby's body sold for medical research in the West. It had been a torturous decision, but her family was so hungry she decided to go through with it.*

Tragically, after the abortion the Muslim surgeon who performed the operation could not stem the flow of blood; she too died. Her body was also sold to **'a useful address where they cut up unidentified corpses to obtain skeletons for export'**.[11] Her husband and children never knew why she had disappeared.

We are repulsed by such stories because we know that there is something more majestic about human beings. These things are degrading to the very essence of our existence.

In Paul's speech to the Areopagus, he was determined to convey the truth that creation was not part of a gigantic experiment by God. We are created for a purpose. Every life is significant because God made us so that we could enjoy a relationship with Him.

'AS A PRODUCT OF CHANCE EVOLUTION, I HAVE NO MORE SIGNIFICANCE THAN A ROCK OR A SNAIL.'

THIRD YEAR PHILOSOPHY STUDENT

Aimless, pointless living was not on God's agenda. Sadly, this is frequently the frustrating experience of so many who keep God on the periphery of their lives. Britney Spears expresses these feelings in Lucky: **'If there's nothing missing in my life, then why do these tears come at night?'**

Nothing can permanently satisfy the emptiness, hunger and thirst that characterises the person who has rejected God and His ways for their life. There can be a temporary anaesthetising of the inward longing, but it can only be cured by the Spirit of God dwelling within the heart of the individual.

Helene Hanff was the fascinating author of 84 Charing Cross Road and other bestsellers. After struggling for years to gain recognition as a writer she was eventually rightly acclaimed for her brilliant, unique style. All she had worked for came her way, but towards the end of her life she reflected on her achievements:

I thought of '84', the miracle of my life. I would never understand. I thought of 'The Duchess', the trips to London, and dazzling moments that had happened to me there. And like a resentful child when the party's over, I thought: 'What have you got to show for it all?'

I looked around my room. The Futura gin bottle (carefully preserved under a bell jar) stood on a breakfront shelf. The leather-bound '84' was up on a bookshelf. A framed photograph of the plaque hung on an alcove wall. In a long storage cabinet, installed under the bookshelves a few years ago, was a videotape of the TV show alongside a large manila envelope full of brochures from the literary tour and the lovely drawings Ena had made for me of Mama Deutsch's flat and Jane Austen's house. On the bottom shelf of the cabinet were the London reviews. 'Trinkets,' I thought sourly, 'and yellowing paper.' [12]

The Art Gallery in the city of Hull contains a painting called A Man with a Muck Rake. It pictures an old man with a small pointed beard scraping on a muck pile with a rake. One hand is outstretched to grasp a bauble in the pile of earth. There is a look of utter glee in his eyes, but he seems unperturbed that his ankle is chained to the earth. Worse still, he appears not to notice that Christ is standing behind him, tapping his shoulder and calling him away from the worthless, passing things of the world.

As human beings we were made for more than that. At some stage in my life my mother let slip the fact that I was an 'accident'. Apparently my parents felt they could not afford another child. However, there is no such thing as an accident in God's reckoning. Each of us was intentionally and uniquely designed by God. The Bible tells us 'we are God's workmanship'.[13] God knows the date of our birth, and the exact time of our death. He was in control of who my parents were, when and where I would be born, the abilities or lack of them that I would have, my racial background and the environment in which I would be raised. Life is short, but significant. And though there are injustices, horrifying inequalities and many unanswered questions in our world, each individual is special, not only to themselves but also to the One who made them. God is not in the business of wasting our time, talents, toil or pain.

His affection is towards us, so we are given abilities to train into skills, personality to mould into character and a spiritual nature which God desires to make alive as He brings us into a relationship of peace with Himself. Once we know Him there is a significance and purpose in all that we do and experience.

'I THINK OF **TRUTH** CREATIVELY.

IT IS **WHAT YOU THINK** IT IS.'

1ST YEAR DIVINITY STUDENT

As Paul explained all this it seems that the Areopagus sat listening. There is no mention of any heckling or distractions. No doubt the council of men had their questions, but at this stage they were able to contain any disbelief. Perhaps it all seemed logical and reasonable to them.

We were created to know God, but our disobedience to Him has separated us from the knowledge of God which should have been our joy and privilege. 'Sin' is the word the Bible uses to describe our insistence on going our own way and doing our own thing. Sin is breaking God's commandments. It has brought suffering and death into the world. It constantly gives the promise of pleasure, but in reality it beckons us to life without God. In his speech, Paul focused on the idolatry of the people, i.e. they were breaking the 2nd commandment.

'Conscience doth make cowards of us all,' *wrote Shakespeare.[14] God has placed in each one of us something that acts like a judge against us. We all know that we are not the people we ought to be. We would love to be truly free, but we don't have the power to do as we ought.*

Nelson Mandela, reflecting on what had happened in South Africa, said, **'Little did we suspect that our own people, when they got a chance, would be as corrupt as the apartheid regime. That is one of the things that has really hurt us.'**[15] *One of Jesus' statements concerning*

Himself was, *'If the Son makes you free, you shall be free indeed.'* [16] Christ is able to give the desire and power to live the lives we were created for. Freedom through a relationship with God does not mean that we can do anything we want, but rather that we can be empowered to start to become the people God intended us to be.

THE TEN COMMANDMENTS

1. You shall have no other gods before me

2. You shall not have any idols or worship or bow down to them

3. You shall not take the name of the Lord your God in vain

4. Remember the Sabbath day to keep it holy

5. Honour your father and mother

6. You shall not kill

7. You shall not commit adultery

8. You shall not steal

9. You shall not bear false witness

10. You shall not covet

Paul told his audience that God's purpose was for nations to seek after Him, which assumes an awareness that God was distant from them.

Today this finds expression in phrases such as, 'There must be something more to life...,' or 'My view of God is...'

Today's spirituality wants a god who doesn't interfere in the lives we have chosen; there is still an acceptance that there is more to our existence than merely the material sphere. P.D. James has a character in her novel Death in Holy Orders who expresses this well: **'People might want the illusion of spirituality. No doubt by and large they believe in God, and the thought that death might be extinction isn't agreeable. But they've stopped believing in heaven and they're not afraid of hell, and they won't start going to church.'**[17]

God wants to re-establish what has been lost (a relationship with God), and bring to life what is dead (true spiritual life). No man-made religion or god has the ability to bring a person into contact with the infinite eternal God who made heaven and earth.

Even the Greek poets expressed something of this, and Paul quoted them. They described people as 'God's offspring'.[18]

Today's writers and poets grapple with the same issues. One month before he died in 1995, Kingsley Amis said, 'There is no point to life, though there is point to art.'

In his book A Passage to India *E. M. Forster wrote: 'Most of life is so dull that there is nothing to be said about it, and the books and talk that would describe it as interesting are obliged to exaggerate, in the hope of justifying their own existence.'[19]*

Perhaps young Anne Frank expressed her hopes best in her 1929 - 1945 diary, writing on 4 April 1944, 'I want to go on living even after death.'[20]

'REINCARNATION IS A NICER OPTION.'

2ND YEAR PSYCHOLOGY STUDENT

The Areopagus was still listening intently. They reacted as if there was little to get too agitated about considering the nature of God, or what it means to be human, and the place of spirituality. But all that was about to change. As Paul explained the good news of Jesus there were going to be reactions and even a refusal to continue listening. There is something so compelling in the person of Jesus that people never remain neutral towards Him. There is always a reaction. People are either drawn towards Him or react, often irrationally, against Him. The Christian message does not only demand intellectual assent. If a relationship with God is the hub of Christian experience, then it will inevitably have consequences. How can a bridge be established between God and us?

'GOD IS THE ULTIMATE AGONY AUNT.'

2ND YEAR INTERNATIONAL STUDIES STUDENT

GOD'S GREAT PLAN

For centuries, it appeared that God was able to overlook the waywardness of people, but He was preparing the world for the unfolding of this great plan to reconcile the world to Himself. The perfect moment came and, in the fullness of time, Jesus was born.

It was a Roman decree that led Joseph and Mary to leave Nazareth and go to Bethlehem, their place of family origin. Little did Caesar Augustus realise that by ordering the world census and insisting on everyone returning to their birthplace he would bring into place the conditions to fulfil Micah's prophecy of 500 years earlier. Micah had proclaimed that the Messiah would come to earth, and one verification of His authenticity was that He would be born in the tiny village of Bethlehem, eight miles south of Jerusalem.

There was 'no room in the inn',[21] so Jesus was to be born and laid in an animal's trough. God was entering our world, but not in a palace, or in front of a television screen. His birth could hardly have been more obscure – what a contrast to His highly public death!

The Bible carries four accounts of the life of Jesus Christ. They look at Him in His role as the Sovereign King (Matthew's Gospel); as the Servant (Mark's Gospel); as the Saviour (Luke's Gospel) and as the Son of God (John's Gospel). They carry descriptions of His relationships with others and recall His teaching in detail. He spoke with authority, though what He had to say was very different from the religious or political teachers of His day. He gave the world a code of living which we find impossible to meet, but which was a description of His own life.

When He taught that we should love our enemies, or pray for those who persecute us, or turn the other cheek when we are hit in the face, He was describing what He had been doing!

The Gospels record Jesus' miracles in historically accurate detail. He had power over the elements, disease, death and even demons. He healed the sick, raised the dead back to life, fed the hungry crowds, calmed the storm at sea and changed people's lives for the good. He even forgave people's sins, something only God has the right to do. He did not spend His life networking and trying to gain promotion or favour with those in positions of political authority. He often met with the underdogs of society and the ordinary people clamoured to hear Him, while leaders feared His denunciation of their hypocrisy.

Jesus invested His life in a few people who were then to take the message of what He accomplished to the ends of the earth.

CRUCIFIXION

As Paul developed the theme of the person of Christ to the men of the Areopagus, he moved on to the issue of judgement. We only have a brief reference to what Paul said, but it is important to realise that judgement not only refers to the Christian belief that there is a day coming when each one of us will appear before God – it also includes God's means of pardon for wrongdoing. It includes the guarantee that all can be well as we pass through death, from life here, to eternity. All of us deserve hell, which is eternal, but heaven is a gift from God to those who will receive Christ, and He even prepares a place there for us.

Christ came to die, and take on Himself the condemnation that judgement should rightly bring to us. The cross of Christ is the defining moment of His work. Jesus repeatedly said that He had been born to die. While people were behaving cruelly, God was providing the world with the means of personally experiencing His great love towards us.

Paul's emphasis on the death of Christ and His rising again is such that it almost appears as if Christ came to do just three days' work! The crucifixion and resurrection is Christ's – and history's – defining moment.

Shortly after appearing at the Areopagus, Paul was to move on to Corinth. When writing to the Christians in that notoriously seedy city, he explained his priorities in the message he was proclaiming. He said, **'I am determined not to know anything among you except Jesus Christ and Him crucified.'**[22] Who Christ was and what He had accomplished was Paul's central theme. That Christ has died for sin and has risen from the dead is the power that can change lives. Paul said to those transformed people who were the Church at Corinth: **'If anyone is in Christ, he is a new creation; old things have passed away; behold, all things have become new.'**[23]

Understanding that Jesus is the Son of God is necessary to be able to grasp what He achieved by dying on the cross. After all, tens of thousands of people had been executed by the Romans on their gibbets. It was not uncommon to see victims agonising in shame as they languished on a cross for days before their chest collapsed and death released them from earthly suffering. They were ordinary people, and in most cases would have died for crimes they had committed.

Christ's crucifixion was infinitely more significant. First, this was a case of the death of an innocent. No one could fault Jesus. Even today, those who want to dismiss Christianity can easily find hypocrisy and sin in Jesus' followers, but not in Him. His enemies failed to agree on their accusations against Him. Secondly, Jesus claimed to be more than just human. The Bible teaches that He is God manifest in the flesh. His enemies accused Him of blasphemy, but He truly is God in the clothing of a human body. God became flesh and lived among us.

His miracles demonstrated His powers to do what only God can. His consistently clean life was open for all to see. When Jesus asked, **'Which one of you finds fault with me?'**[24] there was silence. As the pure Son of God, Jesus was qualified to take the penalty of the world's sin on Himself and pay an infinite price for our sin.

The offences we have each committed against God are sufficient to condemn every individual for ever. The goodness of Christ led Him to go to the place called Calvary, and be crucified there. In the excruciating hours on the cross, God laid on Jesus all our sins. They were abhorrent to Him, yet He paid the full penalty for them. Jesus died for the sins of us all, and for all of our sins. As the Bible explains it He died, **'the Just for the unjust, that He might bring us to God;'**[25] **'He made Him who knew no sin to be sin for us;'**[26] **'By His stripes we are healed;'**[27] **'God demonstrates His own love toward us, in that while we were yet sinners, Christ died for us.'**[28]

The greatest act of love ever shown towards us was when Jesus took the judgement of God on Himself.

God is not a vindictive deity, but He **'so loved the world that He gave His only begotten Son that whoever believes in Him should not perish but have everlasting life. For God did not send His Son into the world to condemn the world, but that the world through Him might be saved.'**[29]

'WHEN I UNDERSTOOD THAT CHRIST HAD ACTUALLY DIED TO PAY FOR MY SIN, I FELT THE LEAST I COULD DO WAS TRUST AND FOLLOW HIM.'

SIXTH FORM STUDENT

▶ RESURRECTION ◀

Luke described the resurrection of Jesus as having 'many infallible proofs.'[30] So for Paul to start explaining the theme of the resurrection was to put him on safe ground. However, to his listeners, the idea of Jesus conquering the great enemy death was ridiculous, and it appears they didn't even hear him out or consider the evidence of its historicity. Given time, Paul would have been able to disarm the critics of the Areopagus by explaining the mountain of evidence for the resurrection, but their unwillingness to believe got the better of them and they heckled him down.

Even today, the idea of Jesus rising from the dead at first appears implausible. Yet, when one attends a funeral, it is hard to stomach the atheist's dream, as Bertrand Russell put it, that 'when I die, I rot'. Perhaps we can better understand his unbelief when we consider that his life was characterised by repeated moral failures. No doubt his conscience could not cope with the thought of judgement to come. Despite that, there is within us a desire for there to be more to life than just our three-score years and ten.

In his final novel about Inspector Morse, The Remorseful Day, Colin Dexter grapples with these issues. Not only does the hero himself die, but, describing Morse and his Chief at a funeral, Dexter writes:

Chief Superintendent Strange ... was the last but one to leave. His thoughts had roamed irreverently throughout the short service, and the superannuated minister's apparent confidence in the resurrection of the dead had filled him more with horror than with hope. He thought of his wife and of her death, and experienced that familiar sense of guilt that still remained to be expiated ... he could think of nothing more detestable than a funeral.[31]

Death and issues of life after death raise big questions in the minds of each thinking individual.

'LIFE IS A FUNNY THING THAT HAS HAPPENED TO ME ON THE WAY TO THE GRAVE. THAT IS ALL!'

STUDENT

EVIDENCE FOR THE RESURRECTION

Paul was convinced that Jesus lived, died, was buried – and rose again three days later.

The Roman soldiers who attended Jesus' crucifixion were professional executioners. They knew what they were doing; they had killed many others before. In fact their lives depended on them completing 'the job'. Normally, to hasten the death of their crucified victims, the leg bones of the individual would be broken. In fact, this was done to the two thieves crucified on either side of Jesus, but He had died before this happened. Centuries earlier, Old Testament prophecy had described the coming Messiah's death, and said **'not one of His bones shall be broken.'**[32]

Unlike the thieves, Christ had suffered spiritually to pay for sin and had then given Himself over to death as He cried, **'Father, into your hands I commit my spirit.'**[33]

Discovering that Jesus was already dead, but wanting to ensure that they had executed Him, the Roman executioners thrust a spear into His side, perforating the pericardial sack surrounding His heart. This prompted the observant comment from the disciple John that blood and water emerged from Jesus' side, an indication of death. Inadvertently the soldiers were again fulfilling a prophecy of old that **'His side would be pierced.'**[34]

When Jesus' body was taken down, it was wrapped in clothes and buried in a previously unused tomb situated near to Calvary. A millstone was rolled in front of the cave, sealed with a waxy cement and guarded by soldiers.

The body lay there until three days later. Then the stone was rolled away, not so much to let out the body, as to let people look in – and see that the body had gone! The soldiers were stunned and invented the story that they were asleep when Jesus' disciples came and stole the body. Nobody seemed to ask how they knew what had happened if they were asleep or why moving the stone had not disturbed their slumber. Significantly, Jesus then appeared to groups of disciples and other people, as well as a crowd of over 500, and showed Himself alive to them all. Even the disbelieving disciple, Thomas, was convinced when he met the risen Jesus, as was Jesus' half-brother James.

It was the risen Christ who changed the fearful disciples who deserted Jesus at the time of His death into bold men who were to preach in cities, towns and villages, taking the gospel to every corner of the earth. They even changed their day of worship from the strict observation of the Saturday Sabbath to Sunday, which they called 'the Lord's day', to commemorate Jesus' rising from the dead.

'I LIKE TO TAKE THE BEST BITS OF EVERY RELIGION, AND THEN JUST DO MY BEST. ONE DAY I MIGHT BECOME PERFECT.'

POSTGRADUATE LAW STUDENT

'JUDGE JESUS'

Paul explained to the Areopagus that the resurrected Christ sits on the bench in judgement.[35] God has appointed a day when Christ will judge the nations and individuals.

In her Year 2000 Christmas Day speech to the Commonwealth, Queen Elizabeth showed that she was aware of this when she said, **'For me, the teachings of Christ and my own accountability before God provide a framework in which I try to lead my life.'**

At the judgement there will be no habeas corpus, no appeal to a higher court, for this is the highest in all of creation. There will be no question of unfairness, for God knows every detail of all the facts, and is too kind and just to pervert justice. There will be no pleading of mitigating circumstances, or a lawyer's spin to enhance the defence. The issue will be decided by what a person has done with Jesus Christ. It is not a case of the good go to heaven and the bad to hell. None of us is good enough for entry into God's holy heaven. The question will be: Has the individual received the forgiveness that Christ has bought? Has the person been set free? Has all that would condemn him or her been forgiven?

Have they trusted Christ as Lord and Saviour? How a person has responded to the grace of God will determine their eternal destiny.

In January 2001 Peter Mandelson resigned from the British government's Cabinet because of lies that had been told. In July 2001, Jeffrey Archer the novelist and politician, was sentenced to four years in prison for lies he told in his libel action fourteen years earlier. Lies keep a person out of government, and more significantly, out of heaven. The Bible teaches that nothing that is deceitful, impure or shameful will enter heaven, only those *'who are written in the Lamb's (i.e. Christ's) Book of Life'.*[36] If we rely on our works to save us we will find they fall short of God's perfect standard. Only faith in Christ can bring about forgiveness and eternal life.

Lord Hailsham, ex Lord Chancellor, said before his death in 2002, 'When I die, and I stand before God in Judgement, I am going to plead guilty and cast myself upon the mercy of the court.' How wise!

Paul knew that it is a living Christ, not a dead idol, who frees and forgives people. It was this he was proclaiming, even if his spirited defence of Christianity was cut short by the derisive heckling of his audience.

'IF ANYONE SAYS THEY ARE RIGHT, AND EVERYONE ELSE IS WRONG, THAT IS WHEN I START TO KNOW THAT THEY ARE TALKING RUBBISH.'
UNIVERSITY LECTURER (WHO FELT THAT THIS POSITION WAS ABSOLUTELY RIGHT!)

Paul had been heard in the synagogue and market place of Athens. Later in his life he would appear before Kings and rulers, and probably before the Emperor Nero. The reaction he encountered at the Areopagus was typical of the way people have responded to the claims of Christ on their lives then and since.

Some mocked at what he was saying, and no doubt this hurt Paul.

Why do people insist on scorning Christ? There is not the same reaction to other religious leaders. I have never heard the name of Moses, Mohammed, the Pope or Buddha used blasphemously, yet it seems there is something in the heart of humans that is anti-Jesus Christ. How sad to use the breath God gives to fight against Him. And yet I am convinced that God's love is such that He can transform the mocker to bring him or her to God.

Some simply delayed their response to what Paul had said. They said they would hear Paul again on the matter of the gospel. As far as we know Paul never again preached in Athens.

It is right to carefully consider Christ, and Christians do not fear being questioned concerning their beliefs. However, God does not guarantee further opportunities to hear the message. There is an urgency about how an individual responds to Jesus. The Bible says that today is the day to get right with God. Why add another 24 hours of living without God, if He is waiting to become the greatest Saviour and Friend now?

We were created to enjoy a friendship with God. It is our wrongdoing which has cut us off from Him. And our sin renders us powerless to become the people God, or even we, want to be.

*Robbie Williams said in September 2000, **'I've fallen out of love with alcohol because it doesn't cover up my inadequacies any more.'** Two months later witnesses reported that he collapsed at the MTV Awards party. His record company said he was exhausted, although newspapers questioned whether this was the full story. We all need supernatural power to be able to overcome our frailties and sins. Once sin is removed, we enter into the freedom of a relationship with our Maker. To merely muse on the possibility of this is to miss out on life's true purpose.*

The book Into Thin Air *by Jon Krakauer relates the hazards that plagued the climbers in the expeditions to Mount Everest during the spring of 1996. In one instance, because of the very high altitude, one of the leaders was in desperate need of oxygen. Though he was surrounded by a cache of oxygen canisters he kept radioing for more because the canisters were empty. They were actually full, but the lack of the very thing he needed so disorientated his mind that, though he was surrounded by a restoring supply, he continued to complain of its absence. Lack of oxygen diminished his capacity to think clearly. The very thing that he held in his hand was absent in his brain and ravaged his capacity to recognise it.*

Christ offers forgiveness from sin, but that sin distorts our view of Christ, who can meet our deepest needs!

'I LIKE THE TEACHINGS OF JESUS AS LONG AS THEY ARE NOT UNDER THE BANNER OF CHRISTIANITY.'

2ND YEAR PHILOSOPHY STUDENT

In the Areopagus there were a number of people who actually believed and asked Jesus Christ to become their Lord and Saviour. We don't know how many, and numbers are not important. God knows every heart and how each one responded, but among those who did believe two people are named. There was a woman called Damaris. Perhaps she is specifically named because she was or became well known. Then there was Dionysius the Areopagite. Whether he was the caretaker of the Areopagus, or perhaps the Chairman, we don't know. Either way, he was a man who had heard many philosophers put forward their views. He would have developed a fair degree of perceptivity. His probing mind would have been able to weigh the pros and cons of each logical structure. And he came to believe in Christ.

Christian experience is received by faith, yet there are solid facts on which that faith is founded. Faith is not a leap in the dark; it is obedience to what God has revealed. God gives faith to those who ask. Dionysius became a follower of Christ after hearing the Christian message just once.

'THE GREATEST DAY OF MY LIFE WAS WHEN THE GOD OF HOPE, LOVE AND PEACE CAME INTO MY LIFE AND GAVE ME ALL OF THESE.'

STUDENT USING GAP YEAR TO WORK WITH INNER CITY KIDS

That still happens today. Liz MacFarlane was a sceptical sixth former. She called herself an atheist and debated the issue with anyone who would listen. She studied zoology at Aberystwyth University and earned a first-class honours degree. During her three years there she never attended a Christian meeting, and she continued her personal crusade against all things spiritual.

She then went to Cardiff University to study medicine. In her fourth year she was sharing a house with a group of other students – all non-Christians. One night the course of conversation turned to religion. One girl said to Liz, **'Oh, you're so anti-Christian and you've never even been to church.'**

Liz was determined to disarm her friend's criticism and approached the elderly couple who lived next door and whom she knew went to church. They suggested the Sunday evening service, but Liz insisted on going in the morning. She went to The Heath, an independent Church with 800–900 in the congregation, where she watched what was going on, but did not join in.

The preacher, Vernon Higham, announced he was going to preach on the Bible command found in Paul's letter to the Ephesians, **'Husbands love your wives.'**[37] It was hardly the most appropriate verse for a single, female medical student.

*But when the whole Bible passage was read, it included the words, **'Do not be drunk with wine, wherein is excess; but be filled with the (Holy) Spirit.'**[38] Suddenly Liz was overtaken by the thoughts and memories of the excesses in her life. She barely heard the sermon, but God was speaking to her conscience and heart. She remained seated at the end of the church service. Someone came and sat with her and that morning she asked Christ to be her Lord and Saviour.*

It was the first time she had been confronted with the claims of Christ on her life, and she believed. She is now married (to a doctor) and is herself working as a General Practitioner in the north of Scotland.

Dionysius and Damaris heard one genuine Christian – Paul – and believed on the Christ of whom he spoke.

As Paul's defence of Christianity was concluding, he said to his audience, 'God commands all men and women to repent.'

'THIS LIFE IS LIKE AN EXAM – IF YOU DO WELL, YOU GO TO HEAVEN; IF YOU FAIL YOU GO TO HELL.'

OVERSEAS STUDENT

To repent means to turn from what is wrong, and trust Jesus Christ in a personal way. God has given us Ten Commandments and we have failed to keep them, but here is an eleventh! If we will obey this one, it will make up for the breaking of the others. Repentance is more an act than a feeling. It is not always easy to measure how sorry we are for sin. However, if there is a willingness to break off from our wrongdoing, receive God's forgiveness, and start following the Lord Jesus, then clearly there is repentance. God will give us both the desire and power to repent, if we ask Him.

God has reached down to us in sending Christ to earth. Jesus suffered on the cross for us. His love to us is such that He will not turn away anyone who comes to Him by faith.

Those members of the Areopagus who actually believed and trusted Christ knew very little of God's unfolding plan over many centuries. Their knowledge of what God is like (one God in the multiple personality of Father, Son and Holy Spirit), or what the Bible contains and teaches, or the life of Christ, or what God has shown us in the Scriptures concerning the end of the world or even life after death, was virtually non-existent. But they had heard enough to respond by faith and receive Christ.

'I CAME TO THE CONCLUSION THAT ALL MY CLEVER ARGUMENTS WERE JUST EVIDENCE THAT I WAS RUNNING FROM GOD...

As they moved on in their life as Christians, they would experience what it meant to have been 'born again' as Jesus expressed it. They would have opportunities to read the Bible for themselves, and have the wonder of God teaching them as they read. They would be able, moment by moment, to talk with God in prayer and discover His interest and involvement in every detail of life.

They probably found as well that, in swimming against the tide of the world's thinking, they met opposition and even persecution.

Jesus never promised His followers an easy life, but He did promise that He would be with each Christian, even to the end of the world. David Livingstone, the missionary explorer, said those were 'the words of a Gentleman'.

Wherever you are just now, you could ask God the Father to free and forgive you, and thank Jesus, the Son of God, for dying and rising from the dead for you. Thanking God and asking that the Holy Spirit will come and live within you for ever, will bring you into a relationship with God.

As you talk to God like this, God promises to answer your prayer and to make you His child for ever. He will guide you through life, and even through death, to be with Himself, for ever.

... EVENTUALLY HE CAUGHT UP WITH ME
AND NOW I WONDER WHAT I WAS AFRAID OF.'

POSTGRADUATE LINGUISTICS STUDENT

For more information click on www.tell-me-more.org

NOTES

1 Stott, John R.W., *The Message of Acts* (Leicester: IVP, 1990)

2 John 11:25

3 *Daily Telegraph*, 20 June 1997

4 Adams, D., *Hitchhikers' Guide to the Galaxy* (London: Pan Books,1979)

5 John 14:16

6 Acts 17:27

7 Genesis 2:7

8 2 Timothy 4:1

9 Galatians 3:28

10 Smith, Wilbur M., *Therefore Stand* (Chicago: Moody Press, 1945)

11 Lapierre, Dominique, *The City of Joy* (London: Guild Publishing, 1985)

12 Helene Hanff, *Q's Legacy* (New York: Penguin Books, 1985) p.176

13 Ephesians 2:10

14 Hamlet, Act 3, Sc.1

15 *Daily Telegraph*, 3 March 2001.

16 John 8:36

17 James, P.D., *Death in Holy Orders* (London: Faber and Faber, 2001) p.18

18 Acts 17:28

19 Forster, E.M., *A Passage to India* (London: Penguin Books, 1924)

20 Peter Kemp, (ed.), *The Oxford Dictionary of Literary Quotations 1977* (Oxford, Oxford University Press, 1977) p.53

21 Luke 2:7

22 1 Corinthians 2:2

23 2 Corinthians 5:17

24 John 8:46

25 1 Peter 3:18

26 2 Corinthians 5:21

27 1 Peter 2:24; Isaiah 53:5

28 Romans 5:8

29 John 3:16–17

30 Acts 1:3

31 Dexter, Colin, *The Remorseful Day* (Macmillan, 1999) p.274

32 Psalm 34:20; John 19:36

33 Luke 23:46

34 Zechariah 12:10; Psalm 22:16; John 19:37

35 Acts 17:31

36 Revelation 21:27

37 Ephesians 5:25

38 Ephesians 5:18